Narcissistic Ex

Lauren Kozlowski

Published by Escape The Narcissist, 2020.

NARCISSISTIC EX

First edition. March 31, 2020.

Copyright © 2020 Lauren Kozlowski.

ISBN: 978-1393181613

Written by Lauren Kozlowski.

Table of Contents

Introduction

If you've picked this book up, it very likely means that you've got a narcissistic ex, which means you've had the strength to leave your abuser. For that, I want to congratulate you - you've done something so powerful and strong, yet you probably don't feel that way. But, just by taking that big, heart wrenching and difficult step in leaving your abuser, you've proven you've got strength within. Understandably you don't feel on top of the world - you've escaped an abusive relationship after all - but let me begin this book by telling you how, no matter how much you can't feel it right now, you're going to beat the narcissist. You've already escaped, you've taken the first daunting step of leaving the abuser. You can do the rest, believe me.

When I say the 'rest', I mean dealing with the aftermath of your relationship. As you're probably all too aware of, a narcissist hates to lose. They won't let you escape without dragging you through hell first. In all likelihood, your narcissistic ex is goading you from afar with a new partner. Perhaps they're harassing you or have a smear campaign going against you. Maybe they're hoovering you up and dropping you back down as it suits them, or perhaps they're stalking you - all of the above are classic 'aftermath' behaviors of a narcissist. They simply can't take the emotional injury of being left, even though it was their own toxic behavior that caused it. It could also be that the narcissist is the one who ended the relationship but is still keeping you around to use as their extra bit of narcissistic supply even if they've moved on with a new partner.

In this book, I want to use my own experiences to help guide you through the anxiety-filled aftermath phase of ending a relationship with a narcissist. My ex was a vile, cruel, malignant narcissist who I was in a toxic relationship with for seven years. The fallout of me escaping the relationship lasted around three more years, during which my ex harassed me, attacked me, stalked me and made me afraid to leave my home. If he found out I was dating someone new, he'd sabotage that by being aggressive with my new partner or contacting them on social media to 'tell them all about me'. He'd flaunt his new relationship in front of me, taking his new partner to the bar opposite my office at work, knowing I'd see them sitting there from my office window. He'd look up at my office window as he sat there with his new victim, waiting for me to spot him. The evil, frightening look in his eye struck fear through me.

I'd get threatening emails, strange notes shoved through my letterbox and glass bottles smashed at my front door. Of course, I knew it was him, but I couldn't prove it. I felt like I was going insane, and like the abusive manipulation would never cease. Often, the easiest thing was for me to cave in and give him what he wanted. Other times, I would ache to be back with him, and yearn for us to go back to the idyllic relationship we once had.

Such are the complex emotions and behaviors that an abusive relationship provokes. You do things that defy logic and completely cast aside your own well-being.

In this book, I want to help you to prize yourself away from the clutches of an abusive ex, using the same techniques I and many other survivors of emotional abuse or narcissism have utilized.

I will discuss the no contact rule, how to stop missing your narcissistic ex, and how to manage their toxic hoovering. I'll also talk a little about narcissistic stalking, and also about the narcs flying monkeys - the henchmen they employ to carry out their narcissistic bidding.

I hope this book provides you with a source of inspiration and motivation when it comes to dealing with your toxic ex.

Chapter One: Why You Shouldn't Go Back To Your Narcissistic Ex And Why You Need To Move On

When I was in an abusive, narcissistic relationship, it took me a few attempts at leaving before I actually left for good. Each time I left, I was always reeled back in by my ex, even though he'd put me through emotional and mental turmoil. People on the outside looking in could so easily question my choices, and judge me for repeatedly going back to a toxic relationship. Of course, unless you've ever been embroiled in an abusive relationship, it's all too easy to pass judgment on this, but at the time, it feels like everyone is mocking your stupidity. If you've experienced this, you'll know how upsetting and frustrating it is - we don't return to abusive relationships because we love being treated like dirt or because we crave the traumatic experiences.

'Why do you keep going back?' was a question I was often asked when I repeatedly returned to the same person who made me feel worthless. At the time, I couldn't really answer it. I'd say I didn't know why, or that I loved him. In truth, I was scared. It was a case of *better the devil you know*; my ex was familiarity, and I was trauma-bonded to him. Being without him caused me unbearable anxiousness and heartache, but there was an odd comfort to it: it was familiar and all I'd known for such a long time. He'd gaslighted me and abused me so much that I had no self-confidence, no real grasp on reality and zero energy to fight his smear campaigns.

It takes a number of attempts to successfully leave a toxic or abusive relationship - rarely is the first time the last time you'll end the relationship. It becomes a cycle of breaking up and making up, only for the same toxicity to again cause you to end the relationship. Even if you're certain that *this time it's for good,* you've possibly found that you invariably ended back in the clutches of your narcissistic partner.

In this chapter, I want to reiterate why this isn't a good idea. This is to lay the foundations for the rest of the book, to make sure you have the right mindset and vision to be able to deal with your narcissistic ex. Getting back with them because it's familiar, a source of comfort or because you're scared of the consequences if you don't isn't *dealing* with your situation. It's prolonging it.

The manipulative, narcissistic and toxic behavior that plagues the relationship you had with your ex isn't something you can fix; I'm sure you've tried. Forgiveness is possibly something you've readily offered your narcissistic ex time and time again, and I'd like to begin this book by explaining why forgiveness isn't something you should consider this time:

It stops you from moving on

When you keep forgiving and getting back with your narcissistic partner, you're letting yourself essentially get hoovered back in. The potential of your relationship is dangled in front of your eyes as you allow yourself to believe that it *might be different this time.* This blinkered view of the relationship makes you unable to see that the narcissist is incapable of real change; the permanent kind of change that will benefit the relationship. You may be offered short-term transformation whilst the narcissist is trying to win you back, but real transformation won't be happening. The narcissist won't be different this time around, and any changes or improvements are fleeting.

You're likely privy to this, as you've been reeled in time and time again by the narcissist, only for them to revert back to their true colors, eventually. Returning to an abusive spouse only results in you placing the emotional burden of forgiveness on your shoulders, feeling obliged to wipe the slate clean so you can 'start afresh'. By providing your support, love, and forgiveness so selflessly, you're rapidly chipping away at your own emotional needs and your self-worth. Moving on starts by cutting the toxicity out and being stronger than your emotional tie to your abuser.

The more times you take them back, the more drained you become.

Narcissists will always attempt (and often succeed) to suck you back in, even long after the relationship has seemingly ended. They'll try to contact you, aim to get you to pity them, or they may do and say things to purposefully make you angry. In a nutshell, they'll try to provoke a reaction out of you. The narcissist will often tell you they have or will change in an attempt to soften you and wear you down.

You need to put yourself first now.

Ironic as this may sound, self-love is actually a narcissist's greatest fear.

Narcissists don't love themselves (as hard as that is to believe). Indeed, they certainly act as if they do; they act like they're above everyone and everything, and they can often come across as being 'untouchable'. However, this is simply the image of themselves that they want other people to see. Narcissists build a false mask - a fake persona of themselves - in order to escape from the feelings of loathing and unworthiness that festers inside of them.

So, when we're solid and secure in ourselves, have the ability to love ourselves and care about ourselves deeply, this creates a barrier for a narcissist to snare us in - it's incredibly hard for a narcissist to capture someone's heart when they're able to show themselves an abundance of self-love.

Narcissists also prey on people that show high levels of empathy. Again, the ability to empathize is mostly lost when it comes to a narcissist, but they view it as the jackpot when searching for narcissistic supply. Being highly empathetic is an amazing characteristic, but it does have some downsides: one of them is that we become more susceptible to narcissists if we have this trait. Highly empathetic people have a tendency to be more empathetic towards other people than themselves, which enables a toxic partner to take advantage of that. In essence, repeatedly forgiving the narcissist by always empathizing with their story or excuses, means repeatedly putting yourself last.

Without self-love, we create an unlocked door to our hearts that the narcissist can enter and leave as they wish. It's time to put yourself first.

You need to resolve any feelings of guilt you have - and you can't do that with your ex around

You need to take care of yourself first-and-foremost from now on. You can't work towards that with a manipulative, toxic ex lurking in the background. I harbored a lot of feelings of guilt and resentment towards myself when I escaped my narcissistic ex. I felt utterly guilty and mad at myself when I thought about all the time I'd wasted with someone who treated me so terribly, yet I was still so bonded to him that I would always return to the relationship. These conflicting feelings ate me up, and I berated myself daily for the poor life choices that I felt I had no choice but to make. I felt so anxious, alone, and heartbroken without my narcissistic ex, but I also hated myself for feeling this way. I was in a cycle of conflicting emotions, none of which were beneficial to me.

Cutting the ties and allowing yourself to decompress, heal and forgive yourself is a huge yet empowering step to take. After being in a toxic, volatile, manipulative and soul-destroying relationship, this is something you owe yourself.

Healing and closure can only happen if you cut contact

Accepting the relationship - and the events that occurred during it - is part of the healing process. You'll go through a myriad of emotions during the break-up and the following months; you'll grieve, you'll be sad, you'll get angry, you'll become enraged at times... all of these things are part and parcel of the healing process. You can't avoid them, and although they're often thought of as being 'negative' emotions, you need to go through them in order to fully cleanse yourself of this toxic relationship and begin to heal the effects from it.

I can admit that I clung on to the break-up for too long, constantly tormenting myself with thoughts like, 'Why me? What did I do so wrong to be treated like this?' I soon come to see that I'd become my own poison. Even away from my ex and free of the relationship, I was still being controlled by him through the thoughts in my head. It wasn't my burden to deal with, although it took me some time to realize this.

When we seek and eventually get closure, we're taking back control, which weakens the grip the narcissist has on us bit by bit. By working towards closure, we begin to understand why the narcissist behaved the way they did and why we were their chosen victim. This, in turn, allows us to drop the guilt and anger we have towards ourselves. Often, I would feel utter contempt and disgust towards myself for being 'weak' and 'vulnerable'. It was only after I fought to heal and get the closure I needed that I came to understand that those weren't feelings I ought to be the bearer of - those were feelings my ex should be carrying around, not me.

Forget the phrase 'forgive and forget' - you shouldn't forget

When I visited Thailand a few years ago, I fell ill with food poisoning. I'd never felt so sick before. I could barely walk, I was constantly vomiting and I couldn't keep even a sip of water down. My stomach ached like I'd eaten needles. I couldn't stop sweating, my insides were on fire with all of the vomiting and my head pounded from dehydration. The cause of this food poisoning? A bowl of spaghetti carbonara.

Since then, I've not touched that dish. The smell of spaghetti carbonara brings back those horrible memories of vomiting and being bedridden in unbearable heat. The idea of putting even a forkful of that pasta into my mouth makes me want to wretch. It's safe to say that I've definitely become averse to carbonara.

My mind and body now associate that dish with danger, horrible feelings and illness, and they're doing their best to stop me from ever feeling that way again.

In the same way, after an abusive relationship, our mind wants to protect us from being hurt in the same way again. So, healing from the relationship and the abuse you went through doesn't mean you need to forget about it. Forgetting about it only serves to compress your feelings about it, which isn't healthy. Trauma affects us all in different ways, and I know that I spent so much valuable time trying to forget the relationship and the horrible memories I had of it when that was, in fact, going to affect me adversely in the long run.

Remembering the relationship will help you recognize the red flags moving forward, and it'll guide you with getting answers about what led you into that type of relationship in the first instance. Also, it's a great way to show you how far you've come and how much you've achieved, and you should want to celebrate that. By not forgetting, you're allowing yourself to have more wisdom when making future decisions. Wisdom gained from bad experiences makes us stronger and better as a person.

I'm going to assume that you're already out of a narcissistic relationship, but I know all too well how easy it is to be suckered right back in by a toxic ex, particularly if the trauma bond is strong. It's very easy for others to say *'just leave them for good'*, or *'get over them - they treated you horribly'*, but they don't understand the grip a narcissist has on you. Often, comments like this can make you simply head straight back to your abuser - after all, no one else seems to understand your situation, and the narcissist can often be the only form of comfort and familiarity when you feel like that.

If you have no one in your life at the moment who'll give you some supportive advice on why you shouldn't return to your abuser, then let me be the voice of reason for you. After all, I've been where you are now. I know the angst of missing your ex to the point it hurts, even when they've treated you so carelessly. I understand the pain of missing someone you know isn't good for you, and I know how lonely it feels when no-one else understands or truly empathizes with your situation. If you're hurting now, I can assure you it won't last forever; you just need to be strong.

I'll list the reasons why retaining your strength is important below:

They won't change

'It won't happen again.'

'I didn't mean to say that.'

'You're too sensitive... I didn't mean it like that.'

'I can't believe you're treating me like this.'

Whatever their excuse or 'reason', what makes you think that they'll change this time?

In reality, they've likely broken any kind of promises they've made you before, such as curbing their abusive ways or not doing the toxic things that drove you away in the first instance. So, this time will be different, according to them... but I can assure you, it won't.

If you're giving your narcissistic ex the platform to explain themselves or to reach out to you, then I implore you to cut this off. If they did genuinely care about you and your wellbeing, then they'd not have treated you so awfully in the first place. To put it in perspective, they chose to treat you like dirt and risk losing you rather than treating you with the respect you deserve. Hopefully, that helps you understand how disposable a narcissist views other people as.

Repeated manipulative, cheating, toxic and abusive behavior isn't a 'mistake' - especially as it keeps happening. Mistakes are actions or behaviors that occur once and are rectified to prevent future occurrences.

The trust has already been broken

Once trust is ruined, it's hard to win it back - even if you do manage to gain trust back, it's never quite like it was before. If you keep allowing your ex to pull you back in as they please with assurances that they can be trusted, you're wasting time trying to glue together a broken relationship when, deep down, you don't know if it can be fixed.

The constant worry of 'what if they do it again? What if it happens again?' will forever be spinning in your mind, which is a horrible way to go through life. Ask yourself, aren't you worth more than that?

The best predictor of future behavior is past behavior

If you let your partner back in after they've lied, cheated, done or said something unforgivable, you're sending a message to them. That message effectively says that you allow multiple chances regardless of how poor their treatment is of you. Now that you've let your spouse know how kind and forgiving you are, they'll see that as a green light to abuse your kindness. If they've messed up repeatedly, how many times do you need to give them a chance to 'make it up to you' or 'prove themselves'?

Once a narcissist knows they can take advantage of your forgiving nature like that, they'll fully capitalize on that aspect of your personality, viewing it as a weakness to be exploited. Invariably, you'll end up back at square one and heartbroken again.

Your time is more valuable than wasting it on a toxic relationship

Think about all the effort and energy you waste going back and forth to your narcissistic ex. This precious time and effort could be used to focus on yourself and working on bettering your own life. Instead of arguing with your ex, fighting with them or trying to get them to understand how you feel, you could be working on yourself: focusing on your craft, your career or getting fit - whatever you need to do to be fulfilled and happy.

I can tell you from past experience that a toxic ex and the heartache they come with is not worth the time, tears, and energy you waste on them.

By getting hoovered back in by someone who treats you so horribly not only diminishes your self-worth, but it means you're effectively settling. Settling for poor treatment. Settling for a lifetime of disrespect and hurt. Settling for someone who doesn't adore you and makes you feel like you're their world (even if they make statements like this, their actions often contradict this.)

To stop this happening, the first thing to do is initiate 'no contact' with your ex. I've been here before. I know how hard it is to do. The narcissist seems to know exactly how to weaken you down and lure you back in. Half the time, I would reignite contact with my toxic ex of my own accord. I'd miss him so much that I'd break my own 'no contact' rule just so I could feel comfort again. Of course, this did me more harm than good, but I'm telling you this so you know that it's entirely normal. Clean breaks are rare when it comes to break-ups, let alone a break-up with a narcissist. With this in mind, I want to help you avoid the heartache of going back-and-forth with your toxic partner in the next chapter.

If your narcissistic ex is the one who ended the relationship, I know how helpless and cast aside you'll be feeling; trying to get them back seems like the only way you'll be able to feel normal again. Yearning for them takes up your entire mind, and you can't stop thinking about them. However, in order to stop feeling this way, you need to trudge through the heartache and maintain the 'no contact' rule. It'll be hard at first. I won't lie to you, but the reward at the end far outweighs what you're feeling now.

I'll cover the no contact rule in the next chapter, but before I do, here's a quick recap of why you should not think about returning to your toxic ex:

1. **It stops you from moving on**
2. **The more times you take them back, the more drained you become**
3. **You need to put yourself first now**
4. **You need to resolve any feelings of guilt you have - and you can't do that with your ex around**
5. **Healing and closure can only happen if you cut contact**
6. **They won't change**
7. **The trust has already been broken**
8. **The best predictor of future behavior is past behavior**
9. **Your time is more valuable than wasting it on a**

toxic relationship

Chapter Two: Going No Contact With Your Ex

Going no contact means just that: zero contact whatsoever with your ex. As I just mentioned, I struggled with this for some time, and I wasn't alone in finding it hard. When I sought out support groups for other victims of narcissistic abuse, I found out just how many of us end up returning to our abuser, and this made me feel less guilty for my repeated returns to the relationship. It's something we all do, and some of the people in that group continue to do so - they're so trauma bonded to their abuser that cutting ties is something they feel is an impossibility.

My ex split my head open by banging it against our front door when we had an argument. I had to go to the hospital to get it glued back together. I was only in A&E for a few hours, but during that time, my toxic partner was messaging me, trying to call me and begging for me to come home. Of course, he was too afraid to come to A&E to see how I was; he was too much of a coward to come and admit what he'd done and take responsibility for it. Instead, he sat at home and manipulated me from afar.

'You know it makes me mad when you do that - I'm sorry'

'I shouldn't have reacted like that but you pushed me too far'

'I should have better control of my temper when you aggravate me like that'

Those were some of the flurry of messages I received whilst I was getting treated at A&E. My head was spinning, literally, and I was in a vulnerable position. I didn't feel like I could reach out to anyone and tell them what had gone on. I had nowhere to go and I also couldn't imagine a life without my abusive partner in it - I felt utterly stuck. The messages he sent me weren't sorry ones at all, they were thinly veiled blameful messages that accused me of being the cause of his violent outburst.

I was so vulnerable, unable to see my self-worth, and worn down, that as soon as I was done at the hospital, I returned home. This shows how traumatically bonded I was to my abuser; going no-contact with him seemed like something I'd never, ever be able to do no matter how horribly he treated me.

There were times when I'd tried to initiate the no contact rule, but I'd find myself checking up on my ex by unblocking his social media accounts and seeing what he was up to. Of course, this would cause me more heartache, especially if I could see he was apparently fine or moving on from me. I'd get myself so worked up and upset, the only thing that would calm me down would be being with the person who caused this horrible pain in the first place. This is a classic case of being trauma bonded to your abuser. You may find that you can relate to my situation here, or that your predicament is similar to the one I had.

However, that trauma bond can be broken; the hard part is that you need to use the no contact rule to achieve that.

So, what is the no contact rule?

The no contact rule isn't a game or a tactic to utilize to get your ex to fight for you or appreciate you more; this technique is often misrepresented as a modern-day dating tool as a way to manipulate your ex into coming back to you.

We shouldn't desire or crave the people who've mistreated us. We certainly shouldn't yearn to have them back in our lives once we've rid ourselves of them. However, a relationship with a narcissist isn't as easy as this - we do find ourselves repeatedly forgiving them, only to be cast aside again. The no contact rule is a solid way to remove our abuser's toxic influence over our lives, so we can live a more stable, happier, and healthier life. Zero contact is the one key that'll ensure the abuser is locked out of our heart and mind, and it'll safeguard us from their spirit-crushing manipulation.

I do understand that it's not feasible for *everyone* to go no contact with their abuser - specifically those who are in a position where they need to co-parent with a narcissist. In these instances, you'll still be able to adapt some of the advice below to your specific circumstances. If you're in a situation whereby you need to remain in contact with a narcissistic ex for legal reasons or because you share children, you should opt for low contact (keep all communication to a minimum - only discuss the bare necessities). You can also utilize a method called gray rock in this instance.

Gray rock means you maintain contact but only offer boring, monotonous responses, so the narcissist has to go elsewhere to get their narcissistic supply. In short, you can't be dragged into their drama or sob stories. If you feel like gray rock is the route you need to go down, here are some tips to ensure it's as effective as possible:

- Never ask questions of the narcissist. Keep it transactional.

- Discuss only 'safe' topics, such as your child or the reason you need to maintain contact. If you have to do small talk, keep it non-emotional - talk about the news, for example. Nothing you talk about should be personal–even if the narcissist is goading you to do so.

- Keep your replies as concise and closed as possible - even use verbal acknowledgments instead of answers; saying 'mmm' or 'okay' instead of rising to the narcissist's bait is preferable.

- Importantly, be sure to keep your head in the game. Don't allow the narcissist to worm their way inside your head, no matter how hard they try. Narcs are renowned for their guilt-tripping ability and have no issues around making you feel bad so that they can get a rise out of you trying to justify or defend your actions. Don't fall into their trap.

Why do you need to utilize the no contact rule?

You may be wondering why no contact is the only way to be free of a narcissistic ex; sometimes you may wish that you could still maintain contact with your ex, and slowly drift away from them, thus cutting out the difficult heartache of no contact. This may have been something you've already tried. If so, you'll be all too aware of how fruitless it is to try doing this; you'll invariably always end up back with your toxic ex.

We need to firmly establish the no contact rule for a number of different reasons, including safeguarding a healthy mind and spirit, especially after enduring a toxic, unhealthy, manipulative, and abusive relationship. No contact allows the time needed to heal from trauma bonds. If we maintain contact with a toxic abuser, this only serves to reinvigorate the trauma bond and goes some way in strengthening it. Zero contact with the person who causes us so much emotional pain also gives us much needed time to grieve the ending of an unhealthy relationship without going back to that toxic person.

The no contact rule is especially needed for those who have been embroiled in a relationship with a malignant narcissist, or someone who has an antisocial personality disorder. These people lay on the more dangerous end of the spectrum, so no contact is a way to ensure your physical and mental health first and foremost.

Toxic narcissists like this often attempt to use hoovering or triangulation techniques to drag us back into the relationship. By establishing and maintaining zero contact, you're stripping the narcissist of that power over you. It's essentially removing yourself from being a source of narcissistic supply in a very unhealthy, derogatory, and non-reciprocal relationship.

How to execute the no contact rule

Complete zero contact requires you to *not interact* with your ex in any manner whatsoever; that means through any medium at all. This includes in-person contact and contact via social media or over the phone. To do this properly and as effectively as possible, you need to remove and block your ex from all social media networks, too. As your ex is likely to attempt to trigger and provoke us through any medium available to them, this is the route you need to go down. It also stops you from being able to see the live updates they're likely giving on their lives after the breakup. They'll probably try to goad you with a new spouse, or appear on social media as being happier without you. Make no mistake, your ex knows you'll see this, and they're doing it entirely for your benefit. Allow yourself the peace of mind of not seeing this by blocking them.

Of course, as I mentioned earlier, I've been there, and I know how hard it is to keep them blocked. Sometimes the urge to see just what they're up to is overwhelming. If you feel like you're going to spy, unblock them or try to find out what they're up to, put your phone or laptop away. I used to put mine in my bedside drawer and find something else to occupy my mind; for example, if I had a strong urge to log into social media and unblock my ex to view their profile, I'd take a deep breath. I'd then turn my phone off and place it in my drawer. Then I'd aim to do something productive to take my mind off it. For example, a phone call I'd been putting off, or I'd take the dog for a walk, or put the dishes away.

During this time, I'd be able to reflect on my urge to see what my ex was doing. I'd try to offer myself as much clarity as possible by reminding myself that my urges weren't going to serve me anything good. I'd think about the hurt I'd been put through already, and how much I'd be hindering my healing process if I unblocked my ex.

You should also block them from messaging, calling us or emailing. For a while, I blocked my ex on everything but email. That was the last thing I blocked, and I prolonged the healing process by allowing my emails to be a way for him to get to me. The emails would range from, 'I miss you, let's meet up', to threatening ones that promised to stop me meeting anyone else. Sometimes, I would reply, too. This, of course, is giving the narcissist what they want. It reaffirms to them that they've still got control over you in some way. As hard as you may find it, block all points of contact. Do it all at once, and don't leave one avenue left open.

Avoid the temptation you have to find out about your ex's life via third parties, mutual friends or any other indirect method. It's also wise to remove triggering photos, as these can lead you to look at these and yearn for the 'good times' or to believe that the relationship 'wasn't all bad'.

In all probability, the relationship likely wasn't all bad, but the bad times shouldn't be as bad or as frequent as they are with your narcissistic ex. Any visual reminders will only serve to remind you of good times, which means you're looking at the state of the relationship with rose-tinted glasses. This is just an illusion. It's not real life. It's a mixture of you yearning for the nice times in the relationship and you wishing the relationship was something it never was. If you don't want to put gifts or keepsakes in the bin (which I highly advise you do, or sell them or give them to charity), then I urge you to put them somewhere out of sight until you're ready to deal with them.

If you've left some form of contact open, or you're required to maintain contact with your ex, always refuse any meetup requests, and make sure you avoid going to any places that your ex happens to frequent. Whilst you may be thinking, 'why should I rearrange my plans to avoid my ex', you should consider this as a way of maintaining your emotional health. You should do anything and everything in your power to protect yourself and your wellbeing, even if it means forfeiting some events and places you used to visit.

Where possible, I highly recommend that you look to cutting contact with friends of your ex-partner, even if this is simply by removing them from your social media. I do understand that you may have formed some close friendships with these people during the relationship with your ex, but when you date a narcissist or toxic person, they're likely to start a smear campaign against you when they see you trying to move on. The friends of your ex will be used as the narcissists flying monkeys, and you won't get any true validation or real support from these people - in all likelihood, they'll side with your ex, which will only add to your pain.

Think of your ex's friends as an extension of the narcissist. Your ex likely views them as *more* narcissistic supply–just another source of attention or resource for them to use when required. They won't see the side of the narcissist that you have, and as such, they're being kept in the 'idealization phase' by your ex. Because of this, they're unlikely to believe your recount of the relationship, the abuse you endured, and could even be used by the narcissist to manipulate or trigger you from afar. I do believe it's in your best interest to cut ties with your ex's friends completely, even if you feel like you won't have any other support around you. This gives you the opportunity to create your own support network that is entirely separate from your ex. There are lots of groups online dedicated to this, as well as plentiful resources and forums online. Escape The Narcissist is a growing platform that is dedicated to this topic in particular, with an ever-growing list of content.

Getting support, friends, and advice online could be your way back into the world of kindness, peacefulness, and empathy. I highly recommend you try to compile your own support network; this also gives you the chance to support others who may be further behind than you in the healing process.

The struggle of maintaining no contact

As I've said, zero contact was a big struggle for me and lots of people in the same situation. If you're finding that no contact is a huge struggle for you to stick to also, there are ways to combat this and make sure you stick to it. Be sure to plan a weekly schedule filled with distracting activities, ideally challenging or pleasurable things. This could mean activities like meeting up with friends, going to a show or the cinema, taking your dog on long walks, and spending time reading self-help books. Whatever you need to do to practice self-care and ensure you're focusing on the right things. Spending time alone isn't a bad thing, as long as you don't get distracted by the thoughts you have of your ex or how much you miss them. You will miss them, but you need to be strong enough to play the long game - in the end, you'll be healed and the yearning you have won't be there anymore. Time alone ought to be spent doing things to nourish you, even if it's watching your favorite movies.

Self-care is an essential thing you need to exercise when you go no contact. As much as you can, ensure you take care of your physical and mental health by exercising, forming a regular sleep schedule and doing things you enjoy doing. I used to enjoy reading, but my narcissistic ex hated me switching off to read books. He called it ignorant and said I was ignoring him when I wanted to relax and get stuck into a good book. He'd prefer us to sit in silence rather than allow me to read a book. For a long time, I had to read in secret, or when he wasn't around. When I escaped the relationship, I was able to read to my heart's content, without jumping when I hear him coming in, or hurriedly closing the book so he didn't know I'd been reading.

Take time to be mindful of your cravings for your ex, which is an inescapable part of the addiction cycle. Whilst they do fade over time, whilst you're enduring these cravings, it seems like the only thing to quell your pain is the toxic relationship. Remember to be patient with yourself - we become literally addicted to the narcissist because of the biochemical bonds created by their cycle of love-bombing, constant devaluation, and surreal trauma. Should you relapse, it's important to thoroughly accept that you've fallen off the wagon. Again, be kind and non-judgemental to yourself if this happens - relapsing is an inevitable part of addiction, and it doesn't diminish the possibility of recovery any less.

As I mentioned before, look up online forums, groups, websites, or blogs that relate to toxic or narcissistic relationships; joining forums like this helps ensure that you've got an understanding community and support network that helps you to remain zero contact. It also allows you to support others who have the same struggles as you. The knowledge and empathy you gain from communities like this can be a crucial aid to your recovery. By entering a community like this, it'll help validate the experiences you endured through the narcissist relationship, and you'll see your story is very similar to others who are a part of the community. If nothing else, a narcissist is consistent in their toxic behavior, and this allows you to create a sympathetic and understanding dialogue with other people in these groups when you discuss your experiences.

Try not to push back on or resist your grief during this period, because it's something you'll have to face at some point, regardless of how much you don't want to. I know it's unpleasant, but the more you run away from negative thoughts and emotions, the more they'll persist, grow and multiply. Be mindful to accept your emotions and the grieving process as a mandatory part of the healing journey.

After offering up self-compassion and forgiveness to yourself, you need to get back on the no contact wagon. I found it beneficial to track my urges to break the no contact rule in a journal. This helped me to curb acting on my impulsive urge to get back in touch. This meant that before I acted on these urges, I'd note down my feelings and urges in my notebook, and I'd give myself an hour or so to collect myself. I'd note why I wanted to get in touch, what I would say and how it would likely turn out. I'd sit and think and gather myself from my pent up, anxious state.

Eventually, this notebook was no longer needed. I began using it less and less until the urge to get in touch was easily brushed off as a bad idea and merely a passing thought - the notebook wasn't even needed at this point. It was then resigned to my bedside drawer. I only found it a few months after I'd last used it, and I'd almost forgotten about ever needing to use it. I read it that day, and I found it cathartic. It showed me how far I'd come from such a low and vulnerable place. It served as something of a cleansing experience when I shredded it to put in the trash. I promise it'll get easier once you allow yourself the clarity of knowing that breaking the no contact rule bears no rewards, only more heartache.

Why no contact needs to remain - always

The demise of a toxic and unhealthy relationship leaves us reeling, often with overwhelming feelings of not being able to cope. Logically, we know we didn't deserve the abuse, manipulation, lies or mistreatment, but we may be tempted to deviate away from logic when our emotions get to such a heightened, overpowering sense of grief.

Trauma bonds keep us emotionally tied to our abusive ex, which is tethered to other factors that the narcissist instilled into us, such as codependency, no self-esteem, low self-worth, and the comfort of the familiarity of the narcissist.

Zero contact is a time for recovering, healing, and ultimately reviving yourself. It's also a time to rip yourself away from the belittling, derogatory, and manipulative grip of your ex-partner. It's a time for you to detach yourself entirely from the toxic person, which allows you to move forward with your life on your terms. No contact allows you to look at the relationship with honesty and integrity from the wisdom of your own intuition, emotions, and thoughts, free from the gaslighting and abuse of your ex.

Keep in mind that anyone who has treated you with anything less than respect and honesty doesn't deserve to be in your life. No contact, the more you continue to practice it, will help you resist the temptation or urge to allow them back into your life.

By establishing and maintaining zero contact, you're ultimately taking back control and hosting your own victory. You're giving yourself the freedom to explore your strengths, passion, and newfound power.

To end this chapter, I'd like to challenge you: I want you to take the first steps in your recovery by challenging you to at least thirty days of zero contact.

This will serve as a detoxifying period, allowing you to begin a regime of self-care and self-love, enabling your mind and body to repair and recover from the trauma and abuse. Remember, if you fall off the wagon, the thirty-day period resets. Be kind to yourself and start again.

Chapter Three: How To Stop Missing Your Abusive Ex

You might be able to fake a smile when your friends and family tell you that you should be pleased because you're not in a toxic relationship anymore. You might even be doing a good job of acting like you're relieved that the relationship is over. You feel like you can't confess that you still desperately miss your ex, knowing that others just don't understand your complex feelings.

Because of this, you may ponder about the fact that you were in emotional pain during the relationship, and you were hurt and upset by the way you were treated. Now that it's over, you feel like you *should* be happy about it - after all, that's what everyone is telling you. *Then why do you miss your ex? What's so wrong with you that you're missing someone who treated you so atrociously?*

First and foremost, there is nothing wrong with you. A toxic, controlling and abusive relationship takes a toll on your psychological health. Missing your source of comfort, even if it was volatile and abusive, is par for the course when it comes to splitting with your partner. A break-up is a break-up, even if the relationship was unhealthy.

To help you understand and legitimize the yearning you have for your ex, I'd like to offer you some reasons why you're missing them. Once I've explained why this is normal and absolutely common, then I'll go on to talk about things you can do to stop missing your ex in such an unhealthy way.

Reason #1 - You're suffering from something called Stockholm Syndrome

Stockholm Syndrome is a condition when the victim of abuse or an extremely controlling environment is made to develop empathy for their abuser. You love your partner so much that you justify the abuse, and can't imagine leaving them. No matter how extreme or disturbing the abuse gets, you can't leave because you're so attached to your abuser. For each abusive deed, comment or action, you'll try to justify it; either by blaming yourself (as the abuser often places blame on you), or you'll feel empathy for the abuser and use their past traumas to explain their vile behavior.

'They had a horrible childhood', 'they were bullied as a child', 'they were treated poorly by their parents', 'they lost their parents at an early age'... the list of justification excuses goes on. Since your ex showered you with love at the beginning of the relationship, you choose to believe that that's the real them: the loving, adoring version. You refuse to believe that the vile, manipulative and cruel version of them is their true character. Even after the relationship has ended, you may still feel this way; the effects of Stockholm Syndrome can be long-lasting, and they don't just fizzle out as soon as you're out of the relationship. Even after you're 'free' of the abuse, the feelings of self-blame, guilt, and empathy for the abuser remain, and until they are acknowledged for what they are, they'll continue to fester.

Reason #2 - You miss the good times with your ex

Abusive partners don't start off the relationship with full-blown abuse. If they did, they'd not be able to snare you in with love bombing, which allows them to have immense control over you as the relationship develops. In the beginning, they often spend quite a bit of time showering you with words of adoration, love, and affection. They make grand gestures that 'prove' their love to you. All of this occurs as part of the love bombing sage, which creates the foundation for which the abuser can take full advantage of your emotional attachment to them.

You believe that those moments of love and adoration from your abuser were sincere, and you can't even begin to comprehend that it was part of a more sinister plan. Because there were good times during the relationship, you believe that the abusive aspect of the relationship can be resolved; that is a blip or a phase. You don't want to face the reality that it's not something that's going to go away, and having to face the fact that your partner won't ever revert back to the person they were at the beginning of the relationship is unfathomable.

Instead, to avoid having to face the painful and heartbreaking truth, you choose to focus on the good times of the relationship. You cling onto the notion that the real them is the one that swept you off your feet in the early stages of your courtship. This is a tactic your mind uses to avoid you having to go through any more emotional injury, and although it can stave off heartache for a short period, you do have to face reality in the end. I believe it's best to do this sooner rather than later.

Reason #3 - Your partner has been through trauma

Life, as you well know, isn't always a breeze. It has its difficult moments. All of us, no matter who we are, have our share of stressful and upsetting experiences. We've all experienced some trauma in our lives, to varying degrees. It may just be that your ex had been through more intense trauma than you. To justify and explain away their abusive behavior towards you, you tell yourself that their vile, narcissistic treatment aimed towards you is just their way of coping with their traumatic experiences.

Regardless of how much trauma anyone has gone through, it's inhumane and unacceptable to make other people suffer for it or to feel responsible for bearing the burden of their trauma. As a loving, forgiving, and supportive partner, you're there to help them through tough times - you're not there to be their punching bag.

Past trauma, under no circumstances, is a way to explain or justify abusive behavior.

Reason #4 - You feel like everything is your fault

In narcissistic relationships, the abuser makes their victim suffer from feelings of guilt and shame. They will purposefully make things look like they're your fault. Because you've been made to carry the heavy burden of blame throughout the relationship, you automatically feel that you're the reason the relationship failed and that you should be ashamed of your actions that have contributed to this.

Even after getting out of the toxic relationship, you may still believe that you are to blame for the break-up and the events that led to it. Because you feel responsible, you miss your ex. You feel guilty for the way things ended, and you possibly think about all of the things you could have done differently to get a different outcome. If you didn't anger them they way you did, if you didn't provoke them so much, or if you just acted the way they wanted you to, then you'd still be with your ex... these are the kind of blameful thoughts that are drilled into you by a narcissist. Because your ex rarely took responsibility for their own poor behavior, you burden yourself with the name of the break-up.

Because you're not placing blame in the right place (with your ex), you feel yearnings to make it up with them.

Reason #5 - You still cling on to the idea that things could have been different

You fell head over heels with your narcissistic ex because of certain qualities you have initially seen in them. They were the kind of person you dreamed you'd end up with; they seemed like they were perfect for you. When they started to show their abusive ways, you were manipulated and gaslighted into believing that their vileness towards you was your own doing.

However, as you fell in love with the attractive qualities they displayed at the start of the relationship, you still cling onto the thought that perhaps things could have worked out differently had you not behaved or acted in certain ways. If you could just have acted in ways that meant they maintained their 'early stages' persona, then you'd have the perfect relationship.

As I mentioned before, these thought patterns are your mind's way of stopping you from feeling any more unnecessary hurt right now. However, in the long run, these blameful, guilt-ridden thoughts are damaging, and facing the truth is a requirement when it comes to getting over the relationship and healing. You need to see the narcissist for the person they truly are, without fogging your view, with self-blaming and excuses for their behavior.

You need to remember that you deserve to be loved back the way you offer your love. It should be reciprocated, respectful, loving, and certainly not toxic.

If you visit support groups and forums dedicated to this topic, you'll find lots of people who are at this stage and are asking *'when will this pain stop'* or *'how long after no contact will I stop hurting?'* One that really stuck with me was the question, *'is it normal to feel this bad after escaping a tortuous relationship?'*

It's a valid question and one that seems to defy all logic. When I read this question, I could tell the poster was desperate - she didn't want to feel this way anymore, and she wanted some answers as to why she felt like she did. I wanted to give her an answer that would appease her and make her feel better.

I wanted to tell her that it was normal, but when I began typing that, it didn't sound right: *it isn't normal,* I thought. Logic would tell you that after escaping horrific abuse and manipulation, you should feel relief.

But, as you likely already know, nothing could be further from the truth.

A relationship with a narcissist is nothing short of an addiction. I found this hard to accept. I detested the idea of being addicted to another being. I felt like it made me sound weak-willed and tarnished me as a 'victim' (another word I was uncomfortable with for a long time). Once I came to accept this, I realized that I needed to literally detoxify my addiction to the narcissist. Like any other addiction, I suffered the withdrawals associated with going cold turkey: the pain, the anxiety, the feelings of insanity, and a constant yearning for my next fix; that next fix being the next contact with the toxic ex.

Going back to the frequent questions I hear like, 'when will I stop feeling so low' and 'when will the pain stop', these types of questions are commonplace in forums and support groups dedicated to narcissistic abuse.

The answer is simple, but it feels like an impossible mountain to climb when you're in the midst of a narcissistic break-up: Simply put, the heartache will ease when you make a conscious effort to regain yourself. You may think I'm being overly spiritual when I say this, or it's a vague way of letting you know 'it gets better', but regaining yourself is the biggest part of getting over a toxic relationship.

I'll explain in the steps below how you can do this.

Step One: get your head around what a narcissist is - understand the person you were in a relationship with. The purpose of this is so you can start to realize that the person who you were with isn't the kind of person who you can have a healthy, honest and loving relationship with.

So, I'll reaffirm to you the answer to the question *'what is narcissism? Why can't narcissists have relationships?'*

A narcissistic personality disorder is defined as a strong presence of grandiose behavior, a noticeable lack of empathy for others, and a constant need for admiration. People who are narcissistic are often seen by their victims as arrogant, emotionally demanding, highly manipulative, and self-absorbed.

Your ex needed to feel power and superiority over you. Narcissists typically give off an aura of being extremely self-confident - even the insular, covert narcissists come across as having an air of self-confidence about them. This projection, however, is illusionary. Deep down, a narcissist is actually fragile. A narcissist will take advantage of any kind acts or empathy you offer them. Even worse, they see your kindness as a weakness–think of the narcissist as the great white shark that can sense blood in the water, except the blood is your kindness.

Because of this, the narcissist cannot have an honest, intimate relationship.

To further cement this in your mind, I'll explain below why this is the case:

They don't really trust other people

In a normal intimate relationship, it's the norm that both partners become vulnerable; vulnerability, of course, requires a deep trust. A narcissist won't reveal their true vulnerability, as they're incapable of putting their full trust in others. Whilst narcissists are renowned for being emotionally stunted, they're certainly as intelligent as their peers. This means they can still logically comprehend the link between trust and vulnerability, but they're aware they're incapable of offering either.

They're always looking for what they can gain out of a relationship

This ties in with the need for superiority and inability to offer vulnerability, as mentioned before. In order to feed their hunger for dominance and superiority, the narcissist victimizes their partner. Heartbreakingly, a narcissist *will* offer love, devotion, and tenderness to you... only to take it away again when their needs require it. This is arguably the most heart-wrenching part of being in a narcissistic relationship; the instability of it all, knowing that any sense of comfort can be dragged from behind you without any warning.

They're full of hostility and anger - and this often turns into violence

The absolute lack of empathy and the deficit of any kind of remorse means that acts of violence can and do happen in a narcissistic relationship. My narcissistic ex had a violent streak, and whilst he would often be apologetic or show slivers of remorse, this was only offered to me in order to get what he wanted. If he hurt me, pushed me around, grabbed me or punched me, any kind of sorry behavior was only given to me to make sure I was pacified enough to still be his source of narcissistic supply.

There's no 'us' when you're in a relationship with a narcissist

At times in a narcissistic relationship, it's hard to gauge whether they're really 'with' you at all. Sure, they're there in presence, but often it can feel like they're devoid of any real attachment to you. The ability to empathize should be a prerequisite in a relationship. Without this key trait, you're never really in a true partnership with a toxic narcissist.

I understand that you're perhaps still at the point where you're hanging onto the idea that your ex can change, but in order to move past the phase of missing them, you need to accept them for what they are. I know your mind may be fixated on finding a way to make it work, and swallowing the truth that it can't work is incredibly hard to do.

This is why you need to purposely get clear on who your ex is. You need to try to be as present and logical as you can when you come to this point, so you can fully process how toxic and bad for you they are. This will help guide you in the direction that you need to take –forward and as far away as possible from this relationship.

After you've taken some time to digest the person your ex is, you can move onto processing the next part:

Step Two: Understand your role in this

This step is in no way whatsoever suggesting you take any blame for the relationship. Instead, this step is about understanding and coming to terms with the fact that you lost yourself in this relationship. Your emotional tie to your ex was likely so strong that they were responsible for your well-being; if they were happy you were happy. If they were upset or mad, you had to endure the result of that, too. This allowed the abusive relationship to gradually wear down your emotions and totally derail your life. All the while, you're clinging on to the idea of this relationship, essentially trying to create sanity out of insanity.

To regain yourself, you need to commit to finding out why you tried so hard to do this.

This is a healthier way of seeking the closure and peace you need instead of forever thinking of all the vile things the narcissist did to you. The pain will only cease when you turn your focus into yourself. This means the self-investigation you're now embarking on pulls your focus away from the toxic ex and towards you. The more time and energy focused on you, the better.

Think of your self-focus as removing your hand from a burning flame. Once you do this, of course it'll hurt and be overwhelmingly painful. However, the agony of that is only relieved by taking your hand away from the burning flame in the first place. Once the hand's away from the flame, healing can begin. You must remove yourself from thoughts of the narcissist and focus them towards yourself, otherwise, you're keeping your hand hovering over that burning flame, which is only going to worsen the wound.

Whilst step one, understanding and accepting that your ex was a narcissist, is undeniably vital in your healing journey, you can't stop there. You must move on to the second step of focusing your time, energy and resources onto yourself. You can only dwell on the narcissism for so long; after all, what you focus your energy on ends up being what you attract.

Your goal from the two steps here is to curate a newfound reality of truth, empowerment, self-love and, ultimately, freedom. By doing these things, you arm yourself with a new arsenal of boundaries that make you a negative match for a narcissist.

These two steps combined lead to acceptance, a crucial ingredient in the path to overcoming this.

I penned this book because I know how it feels to helplessly miss someone who is so toxic and bad for you. I understand how confusing, frustrating, heartbreaking and overwhelming this time is. I know how easily it can be to drift away into sentimental memories, to pine for that time in your life and wish you were back there in that exact moment.

I know what it's like to give someone chance after chance after chance, each time hoping that this is the time it'll be different; all the while knowing deep down that I'll end up hurt yet again. Time and time again, I put myself through the angst and torment, hoping that this person would become who I needed and I would one day satisfy them fully, so they wouldn't feel the need to treat me so horribly.

I know how it feels to hear from other people that your ex loves you, and they miss you–and how easy it is to be hoovered right back into a relationship (I'll talk about this more in the next chapter). Sometimes it can just hit you out of nowhere, the intense feeling of wanting to run back to them.

When I escaped my narcissistic ex for the last time, I was utterly depressed. I focused on the pain of missing him, being angry at myself and feeling a huge amount of guilt. I didn't use my time to build up myself or practice self-care, so I wasn't getting any better. I felt powerless feelings instead of shifting my focus into the right places.

The perfect mantra for this time in your life comes from the Dalai Lama: 'Remember that sometimes not getting what you want can be a wonderful stroke of luck.' In this instance, when you've escaped a narcissistic relationship, you're incredibly lucky - even if you don't see it yet.

Chapter Four: Understanding Hoovering

'Hoovering' is the term used when a narcissist tries to reconnect with you after a period of separation. Often, this occurs after a long time of silence between you and your ex, and can often happen at times when you're seen to be attempting to move on or get on with your life.

If you're the one trying to initiate contact and reconcile, it makes it more likely (although it's not *always* the case) that the narcissist will simply devalue and discard you. Should this not be the case, it's usually because your toxic ex still wants something from you, where they may not be getting it from other resources. For example, possessions, money, contacts, status or sex - but it's just because their other supply sources are momentarily scarce or low.

Plenty of victims of narcissism think, 'why won't they ever leave me alone?' and 'will it ever stop?' Then, on the other hand, many victims have been incessantly refreshing their emails, checking their phones and social media anxiously hoping that their narcissistic ex will contact them. After a relationship with a toxic person, it's very common that you'll fear and dread the possibility of being hoovered, and then, at other times, you'll feel like your heart is being stabbed if you don't receive it.

Hoovering can occur even after your ex has moved on with someone else. The fact that they have a new partner is often seen as insignificant by the narcissist when they come to attempting contact. Even if the narcissist is seemingly loved-up, happy and in a committed new relationship, you know their true colors; that doesn't prevent them from trying to incite a reaction out of you. Their sheer lack of respect for those around them, particularly those who provide them with narcissistic supply, is nothing short of abhorrent.

The way they parade a new love interest in front of you in order to hurt you, the way they show you just how happy they are without you, and how they treat their new spouse so much better (*which they don't*) are all manipulation tactics. They're essentially bait thrown out by the narcissist to try to get you to bite.

There are lots of 'why's' when it comes to understanding hoovering. Why do narcissists–even if you don't respond at all–still try to see if you'll take the bait? Why do they come up with see-through excuses to contact you, only to attack your perceived weaknesses, such as guilt, or defending yourself against manipulative lies? Why does this person possess the ability to rile you up, confuse you, hurt you and have such an impact on your emotions?

Why are you drawn back into the cycle of 'I want you,' only to be repeatedly devalued and discarded? Why doesn't the narcissist's recollection of the toxic, torturous relationship match yours - they are either often sentimental or blameful when they offer up their thoughts on the relationship.

You may have even noticed that it only takes one reply or response to a narcissist's attempt at contact for them to disappear all over again - leaving you head-spinningly confused and naturally upset. *Why would they reach out only to leave me helpless yet again?*

So, why do narcissists hoover?

The answer lies within the fact that narcissists are emotionally empty voids. They need their fix of narcissistic supply in order to emotionally exist. They have a sadistic need to know that they're affecting someone, or have certainty that someone hasn't gotten over them. To a narcissist, the knowledge that their ex is still at their beck and call, or pining after them, allows them to rest easy knowing they have them as a back-up source of narcissistic supply. Hoovering allows the abuser to know they have their prey still 'captured' and it's there waiting for them when they need to 'feed'.

Like a victim is addicted to their abuser, a narcissist is also addicted - not to the person, but rather to the narcissistic supply that person provides. It's not the person who's important - in fact, it doesn't matter where their supply comes from, as long as they get it. Narcissists tend to keep various sources of supply as their backup, ready to utilize when needed.

The worst possible insult to a narcissist is when their ex levels up after the break-up, truly detaching themselves from the toxic relationship, fully healing. When a victim can reach the point of knowing that the reality forced by the narcissist isn't a reflection of true reality, this strikes fear into the narcissist.

There is possibly no threat more feared by the narcissist's ego than being considered insignificant and unimportant. Because the narcissist has no way of validating or sustaining their own emotional well-being, people opting to bow out of the narcissist's game of manipulation and refusing to be involved in their game playing only goes to confirm what they dread: the idea that they're unlovable, abandoned and inferior.

It's this dreaded fear that the narcissist has been trying to squash all this time, with their controlling, punishing and manipulative strategies. Their carefully crafted game of power is a way for the abuser to ensure they never feel those feelings of inferiority.

When this invariably fails, the narcissist's warped perceptions then generate the devaluation and degradations that you've had to put up with. The devaluation of you is a direct result of the narcissist's projected wounds.

The narcissist's apparent despising of you, the malicious abuse, the cutting put-downs and the toxic behavior they exhibit are all to do with the abuser attempting to destroy the parts of themselves that they detest; the parts of themselves that they've decided you represent. They've assigned their innermost hatred of themselves into physical form, and that's you.

It is bewildering that someone, even after committing such hurtful and traumatic behavior, would want to hoover someone up, again and again, emotionally tearing their way back into your life shamelessly, like they've done no wrong.

As shocking as it may be to discover someone as brazen and remorseless as a hoovering narcissist, it's important to understand that the narcissist's fuel–the feeding of their false self–is the only thing stopping them from being confronted by who they truly are, and being tortured when faced with their real inner-being.

Hoovering isn't about love or missing you; not in the slightest. It's a narcissist's necessary survival tool for their frail ego. Everything and everyone is simply something to serve their needs. To escape hoovering, you need to exorcize the narcissist from your being.

Exorcizing the narcissist out of your heart and mind comes from the true detachment that you get from detoxing them from your system. The goal here is to get to the point that you honestly couldn't care less about your ex or what they're up to. Instead, you'll be busy expanding yourself and your life, building something fulfilling for yourself and your promising future.

Ridding yourself of the narcissist and fully detoxifying from them is the best way to stop catering for the narcissist, and allowing yourself to be hoovered at their whim. It also, eventually, allows you to be free of the obsession about whether they'll get in touch with you again or reply to you reaching out to them.

Of course, the go-to human urge before embarking on genuine self-recovery is to retain *hope* - despite repeated evidence that proves otherwise - that your ex has now reformed and will finally stop their vile behavior. It's also very common to - when you don't receive a satisfactory or genuine 'sorry' from your ex - to become enraged. You'll try to fight for some accountability from them, and perhaps even try to force your ex into being the person you met at the beginning of the relationship (before their mask slipped).

Any attention at all that you give to your narcissistic ex (or any more chances you give them), is only offering the narcissist more narcissistic supply. In their head, they think: 'My ability to affect someone else and take their energy makes me significant.' And so the cycle will continue.

Hoovering plays a big part in the cycle of abuse, as often can violence. The cycle of violence in this situation can be explained like this:

It begins with a period of calmness. Then, tension will begin to build, and like a pressure cooker of toxicity, something has to give. Once the tension comes to a boiling point, then abuse occurs. Invariably, reconciliation takes place after this, even if it's not immediately. Then this is followed by a period of calmness, allowing the cycle of abuse to continue all over again.

The key thing to note here about this is that the only abuse intensifies as it goes round in its loop. As it goes on, the cycle becomes tauter and the frequency only escalates.

As obvious as it is to say, it's worth remembering that narcissist's don't tend to learn by their mistakes - primarily because they don't take on board that they're in the wrong. They don't offer genuine remorse, and won't be held accountable for their misgivings. This makes them incapable of real change. Rather than listen to the reactions of those around them and use that to reform their atrocious behavior, they build bigger defenses and feed their inner monster even more. The false self of the narcissist can't take being held under scrutiny, because it treads on their ego.

When the victim is totally battered down, unable to offer up much to the narcissist, they may 'make up' with their victim unauthentically. There were times that I had apologies thrown at me in the form of 'I already said I'm sorry, why isn't that enough? Why do you keep going on?' Once this is accepted (or not), the abuser can then continue on with their toxic business as usual. This is especially the case if the victim has crumbled boundaries and shattered self-respect - the narcissist thrives on the emotional helplessness of the victim.

If your boundaries are getting stronger, but are not yet at a solid point, the narc will finesse their hoovering technique - strengthening boundaries are a big red flag for narcissists, and they know they need to up their ante when their victim is regaining their emotional strength. They'll try to appear utterly repentant, make promises they know will strike a chord with you, and do whatever they need to in order to lure you back to them.

Then, heartbreakingly, if you 'crumble' and allow yourself to be hoovered, you'll be horrifically punished for being so easy and 'pathetic' (a word favored by the narcissist). Should you begin to attempt to put boundaries in place, it's only a matter of time before the narcissist catches onto this and makes moves to ensure that the rug is pulled out from under your feet. The previous 'remorseful' and 'reformed' narcissist will transform into, 'Who do you think you are, trying to get one over on me? You can't try to hold me accountable and think that's okay.'

The remorse and promises they made you? It'll be like it didn't happen; in all likelihood, it'll be used against you to gaslight you: 'I never said that'.

As the cycle of abuse goes on, leaving the narcissist and then returning (especially if the narcissist has had to really fight for your compliance this time) means the cruelty will escalate to horrific levels.

Every time I returned to my abusive ex, it got more and more horrendous; the manipulation, the lying, the gaslighting, the aggression, the violence, the taunting, the isolation... everything that was already toxic only turned even more toxic. Any respite I may have gotten never lasted too long. From being a part of many abuse forums, and talking to other people who were and still are in the same situation I was, I know that this happens time and time again in almost every abusive relationship.

I have asked the question in various narcissism and abusive relationship groups and forums: can an abuser really change or reform? And each time, from numerous survivors, the answer has been a defiant 'no'.

I have never heard of a narcissist or sociopath, both of whom are capable of unimaginable pathological acts, who have reformed and genuinely acknowledged their heinous behavior.

Even if they wanted to, the inner fears, wounds and fragile ego that drives the extreme behavior exhibited by the narcissist would prevent them from reforming.

A narcissist's entire life is built around avoidance of confronting their true self and their inner fragility, so this makes true change nigh on impossible for them.

Hoovering Tactics

From my own experiences with hoovering, and from the stories I've shared with other survivors of abusive relationships, I've been able to compile a list of the commonly used hoovering tactics.

Hoovering Tactic #1: Promising you whatever you want

I had the apologies, declarations of commitment and promises to treat me so much better for the rest of our lives... whatever my ex thought I needed to hear in order to successfully hoover me back in. For a long time, whilst I still clung onto the hope that things would one day get better, these false promises lured me back into the toxic relationship.

I recall one occasion where my ex promised me he was being faithful from then onwards; he assured me he only ever cheated because he didn't think I loved him and that he wouldn't ever do that to me again. I should have known that this was just another lie to hoover me back in because I asked him if I could look through his phone to see if there were any messages or calls that would upset me if I looked. He refused to show me and assured me that there was nothing untoward on his phone.

In his words, 'If you look through my phone, even though there's nothing bad on there, our relationship is finished. We need to move forward with trust - looking through my phone would mean we're moving forward without trust.'

He convinced me to trust him. He was utterly believable. But if you fast forward to two nights later, he went out on a date with another woman, who he'd been messaging for a while behind my back. I only found this out after the relationship had ended, and this woman and I (one of the many *other women*) met up and exchanged our stories of a toxic relationship with this man.

Hoovering Tactic #2: Going to any lengths to persuade you

Another common hoovering phrase is 'I swear on your life', or if you have children, the narc will swear on their lives, too... regardless of whether they're telling the truth or not. My ex even allowed me access to his social media by logging in on my computer and offered me his email password to check his inbox if I was feeling insecure. Whilst I declined his offer for the password, I couldn't help myself from double checking the social media profile he left himself logged into on my computer. To my surprise, his inbox had a message in there about me, sent to his friend. It was gushing about how great our relationship was. At the time, I didn't consider the idea that the message had been sent with the intent of me seeing it; that it had been sent with the sole purpose of pacifying me.

The fact that his social media seemed squeaky clean also allowed me to be less concerned about his wandering eye. However, as I came to find out, the profile he allowed me access to wasn't his only one. He had a number of other email addresses, social media profiles as well as two mobile numbers.

Hoovering tactic #3: Pretending to be supportive

Hoovering is most likely to happen just when you start to find success, happiness or your inner peace. Your ex may claim they want to be supportive of your new endeavors and even express a seemingly genuine interest in them. However, once you're back in the clutches of your abuser, they'll unveil their true colors (yet again).

The narc will begin sabotaging your progress with criticism, scathing put-downs of your positive endeavors. Even if they do this covertly, trying to use humor and sarcasm to devalue your progress, they'll still wear you down, piece by piece.

One time, when I left my ex, we'd not spoken for around three months. I was on my way to recovery, and I'd even applied to do a part-time media course. I was slowly becoming a bit more confident, and the media course isn't something I would ever have been able to do if I was still with my abusive ex; he would accuse me of having an affair with someone there, or remind me that he thought I was incapable of being any good at something like that.

However, just weeks before I was due to begin my media course, I had a knock at the door. I didn't expect it to be my ex, as we'd not spoken for a while, and the last time we had, he'd been absolutely horrible to me. I answered the door, and staring sadly back at me was my ex. I was struck with fear and trepidation - *why was he here?*

He handed me a piece of paper and told me he'd broken his phone and hadn't been able to get in touch. He said he'd just bought a new phone that day and would like me to have his number - just in case. He told me that he's there if I want to text him and that he's missed speaking to me.

I took the piece of paper, in a daze, and he said goodbye. I was almost out of his clutches... but he managed to reel me back in. He seemed kinder and somewhat sad when I spoke to him, and seeing him brought back feelings. I texted him that night.

Over the course of the next few days, we chatted to the point where we decided to meet up. When we did, I told him about my future plans, and let him know about the course. He told me that it was good that I was going to do something I was interested in, and said it would be great for me to get out there and meet different people.

Fast forward a week, my ex was back in my life and we were a couple again. Of course, by this point, he mentioned he didn't want me to do the media course. He said I was too old to be doing it, and that I could find out everything that course teaches on the internet. He said I was only wanting to take that course to meet someone new, and now that he was back in my life, I didn't need to go on it. He made me feel stupid for even considering going on a course, and so I withdrew my application. I didn't end up going.

Hoovering Tactic #4: Big romantic or 'thoughtful' gestures

The letters through the door, the flowers sent to my workplace, the romantic gestures and thoughtful acts that my ex showered me with during some of the hoovering phases were all manipulation tactics. One time, when I was back at my mother's house, he sent flowers and perfume, but got them delivered at a time when he knew I'd be at work. Of course, he knew my mother would pick them up and this was his intention - to win others round and use them to help him hoover me back in. Another time, he got a pizza delivered to my house - but not just any pizza. He'd got the takeaway to make the pepperoni on the pizza in the shape of hearts, as well as write 'I love you' inside the cardboard pizza box.

Whilst this can leave you all warm and gooey at the time, it's just another ploy to mold you back up, so they can squash you back down. The narc needs to know they can have you when they want, even if it takes a little more effort during the hoovering stage.

Of course, he didn't let me forget about these gestures; he would bring them up frequently, mentioning that I'd never do something so thoughtful, and remind me how lucky I was to have someone like him. However, the gifts that were given to me during the hoovering stage often got broken or taken away from me when he got me back in his grip. The perfume would be smashed and the gifted necklace would be ripped straight from my neck.

Hoovering Tactic #5: Inciting your defensiveness

My ex knew how to get to me. If we weren't talking, and I was trying to get on with my life, he always had a trick up his sleeve to get to me. Even if he was blocked, he'd still find a way to get in touch and rile me up like he knew he could. For example, once he used his friend's phone to message me to say he knew I was dating John (I've just made up that name to avoid naming the real person), and that he knew I'd been seeing him even throughout mine and my ex's relationship. He ended the message with the line: 'I hope you're happy with him and treat him better than you treated me'.

This incensed me. I immediately unblocked my ex, and messaged him, asking where he got this misinformation and questioning why he thought I'd ever cheated on him.

I took the bait - hook, line, and sinker. Of course, my ex knew I hadn't cheated, and he knew I wasn't dating John - it was all a big manipulative ploy to strike my defensiveness and get some satisfaction from knowing he could still get to me.

Hoovering Tactic #6: The 'nothing's happened' act

Even if your ex has moved on, has 'committed' to someone else or not spoken to you for a long time, they can often utilize the 'nothing's happened' tactic when they try to hoover you back up.

One time, my ex ignored me for eight weeks, had used his friends to manipulate me from afar, and created a fake profile online in order to trick me into going on a date with 'him'. Still, without any remorse or guilt, he tried to return into my life as if nothing at all had happened. He denied creating a fake profile and using his friends as ammunition against me, and his whole demeanor said: nothing has happened, get over yourself.

This made me wonder, am I being paranoid? *Am I being dramatic? Is it really not as bad as I made it out to be? Am I being a drama queen?*

Of course, I was being hoovered up with gaslighting, and I began to think I was going mad - and my ex gladly helped me turn that thought into a genuine belief.

Hoovering Tactic #7: Hoovering you when they've got someone else and/or wanting to be 'friends'

No matter how loved up they seem, or how many texts they send to you to say how happy they are with their new spouse, this won't stop them from their abuse from afar.

Your ex might send messages out of the blue as if you were 'friends' or someone who 'checks in' from time to time. They'll often dismiss any notions that the relationship was toxic, you shouldn't be keeping in touch, etc. Invariably, the conversation turns towards what you're getting up to, who you may be dating or the relationship you once shared with your ex.

Hoovering Tactic #8: Using your abundance of compassion and empathy against you

This can be especially true if you share children with your ex, but even without the presence of children, a narcissistic ex will always bank on your compassionate nature to worm their way back in. My ex would even get in touch to say he missed the dog, how it was unfair that I was keeping him from something that was 'equally his'.

He would also go on to mention things like ending his own life, doing self-destructive things or threaten me directly by saying that anything bad that happened to him was my fault. He even once got himself checked into A & E after an overdose and had the nurses call me with the news; I was dubious about this at the time, but of course, I was concerned, and I went to pick him up. Looking back now, I can't imagine this being a real suicide attempt - he would never end his own life, and I very much doubt he genuinely overdosed.

Hoovering Tactic #9: Ridiculous messages that clutch at straws

My ex, when all else failed, would message me with odd requests, such as his watch back (that I didn't have), insisting he'd left his driver's license in my handbag so needed to come to get it (he hadn't) or that he'd accidentally gotten a package sent to my mother's address, so needed to collect it (how was this even possible?!)

Of course, these were all him clutching at straws when all other hoovering attempts had finally begun to fail.

Random, see-through, emotionally manipulative messages can also include the use of special events, anniversaries, pretending to care, or using emotive nostalgia such as: 'Please let your mother know I wish her a happy birthday / send your cousin my thoughts before they go for surgery / I hope your niece enjoys her first day of high school.'

Or it could be things like 'Are you going to my sister's 40th party? I hope to see you there.' Or, the especially manipulative, direct to the point messages like 'I'm stood in the place where we first met. I wish you were here.'

If you've been hoovered, you'll relate to these common, manipulative narcissistic tactics.

What I must mention here, is that it's essential to understand that hoovering is not a show of love or a compliment from your abusive ex. When a narc is feeling low on supply and needing a pick-me-up for their fragile ego, any source of narcissistic supply is considered fair game. Instead of dealing with their own inner hollowness and pain, the narcissist will (and I guarantee this) pick up the phone to numerous people who they can suck some narcissistic supply from. You're simply a way for the narcissist to avoid being confronted with feelings that'll deflate their ego and strip them of the power they have - you're not something they can't live without, even if they tell you that.

To reiterate, there's nothing 'caring,' 'loving,' 'loyal.' or 'romantic' about hoovering.

Have you received a message from your narcissistic ex out of the blue, even after you've not spoken or been in touch for a length of time? Did it read something like: 'Hi. I just needed to message you to let you know I'm thinking about you, and I would like to tell you I'm sorry. I miss you... etc, etc.'

If so, let me translate that for you:

'It's me (again) ... it turns out that the other source of narcissistic supply I horribly discarded you for wasn't all that. Of course, they're still in the background, but I'm currently going through a temporary drought of admirers and sources of supply. I either get bored with them, drop them for something better, or they figure me out. So, I was putting the feelers out with you to see if I can lure you back with some of my hoovering tactics. Remember, where I drop in and out of your life, acting as if nothing has ever happened? You can stroke my ego, I'll wreak havoc and destruction - but I'll still be on the lookout for more supply. Is that a deal?'

Why are you susceptible to hoovering?

Narcissists can sniff out our weak spots and they utilize them for their own wicked gain. It's all part and parcel of their disorder–to use people's character traits (generally the good ones, like compassion and empathy) against them.

The most common thought patterns and traits that leave us more open to being hoovered are as follows:

Feelings of over-responsibility

It's likely if you struggle with feelings of being over-responsible for others in your life, and you haven't yet recovered enough to prioritize the responsibility you have for yourself, that you're susceptible to hoovering. Being manipulated by guilt, or the burdensome feeling that it's your role to help. The narcissist will try to pull on your compassionate heartstrings, make no doubt about that.

With a lot of victims of narcissism, they have a deep-seated wound that allows them to be more susceptible to hoovering, which makes them feel like they have to be the caretaker in every situation. This has likely developed from a very young age due to the circumstances they had growing up. Often, they feel that other people's issues are either their fault, or it's their duty to fix them.

I had a malignant narcissist in my life growing up, in the form of my father. My mother was extremely vulnerable, and as such, I took it upon myself, even as a very small child, to be the best caregiver possible for her. I would blame myself if she was emotionally or physically hurt by my father, and felt sole responsibility for her well-being. These feelings of responsibility stayed with me until after I left my narcissistic ex, and I was finally able to address these wounds that began in early childhood.

When you feel the heavy burden of being responsible for others for your entire life, it can be hard to shake this. It's so important to keep this knowledge at the forefront of your mind, however, especially when breaking away from a narcissistic spouse.

Believing that the narcissist is your 'security' and your validation that you're worthy of love

If you feel that your emotional survival, feelings of security and well-being are provided by the narcissist, you're more susceptible to the narcissist's untrue promises and assurances that they'll be the provider of those things.

If you're carrying the idea that you need to earn other people's approval in order to feel worthy or validate your purpose, it's likely you're low on self-love and worthiness, and any words of love, commitment, adoration, and kindness means you're more susceptible to going back to your toxic ex. Because you're so desperate to find some worthiness in yourself, you won't take your ex's words for the empty, manipulative lies they are; you'll blindly take them as the gospel truth.

The belief that you need to justify yourself

If your sense of self and worthiness depends on what other people think about you, then you'll forever be trying to verify your integrity and trustworthiness to others. This means the narcissist can easily hook you in with accusations that they'll know you'll feel the need to defend.

The narc knows you'll bite when you feel persecuted, distrusted and that they'll get a rise out of you when your integrity is in question. These are some of our core internal wounds that keep us in the narcissist's clutches.

Hoovering can also happen in reverse, too, and it's something a lot of victims of abuse have done; meaning that the narc has already devalued, then discarded you, and are refusing to answer your attempts to get in touch with them.

This, as you may know, can make you feel utterly panicked, anxious and full of terror. This reverse hoovering doesn't serve anyone but the narcissist - please bear this in mind if you're feeling the urge to reconnect. Know that the narcissist knows you're hurting, and their lack of contact is only so they can worsen your wounds, making you weaker and weaker - which is great news for them if they decide they need you for any more narcissistic supply.

I want you to know that, even if you get hoovered back in (which, during a break-up with a narc, is inevitable), you're not back at the starting line. Each relapse that leads you back to your toxic ex is another step closer to that *final* break-up - the one where you fully know that in order to heal, you need to fully set yourself free.

Chapter Five: Narcissistic Stalking

Narcissistic stalking is a course of conduct the narc uses to strike fear into their victim, assert their power and ensure they're not letting their source of narcissistic supply slip away. The narcissist utilizes intimidation and elements of control in order to have the desired effect with their stalking. They want their victim to feel vulnerable and exposed, by stripping them of their security and privacy. Stalking can occur before, during and after separation, but the time where it's most lethal is after you've separated with the narcissist. Common examples of stalking are:

Unwanted and or / frequent phone calls and texts

The stalker getting mad or upset if communication isn't responded to quickly

Interrogating questions

Insisting on knowing who you're with/dating/friends with

Disallowing you from having private conversations

Not allowing privacy, opening your mail or checking your phone

Going through your purse/bag/handbag

Having other people keep 'an eye on you'

Having other people tell them your movements or whereabouts

Following you, or being in places they know you'll be

Turning up unannounced

Turning up at your workplace uninvited

Putting rumors or private information on social media/ internet

Uploading private pictures on social media / the internet

'Catfishing' you - pretending to be someone else to gain contact with you

Stalking isn't necessarily a hooded figure following you home in the dark or some stranger who appears everywhere you go; stalking isn't as black and white as that (despite what movies or the news tells you). Narcissistic stalking isn't something I've seen much of in terms of available reading materials or resources, yet it's a prevalent thing I've heard from many other survivors: their ex stalked them after the break-up.

I want to bring light to this topic, as I believe it's dismissed or ignored far too much when it's such a frequent occurrence. More than that, I want to make you more aware of this as a possibility, and ensure that you're alert to the dangers in order to keep yourself as safe as possible. I want to talk about the mistakes and mental blind spots that can blinker you to the true dangers of this kind of situation which can lead you to walk straight into the narcissist's line of fire. Understanding more about this might save your life - even if you don't perceive there to be that much of a danger from your toxic ex - but it's this way of thinking that allows a narcissist to execute some dangerous behaviors.

If nothing else, I want this chapter to just get you thinking about the hidden dangers associated with splitting up a narcissist, and how common it is for a narcissistic ex to stalk their victim in order to retain control. Ideally, I want this chapter to make you more aware, alert and prepared for any post-breakup stalking behavior and know how important it is to never just brush it off or avoid confronting it.

Rationalizing your ex's stalker behavior is something all victims of this type of stalking have tried to do. Some exes who turn into stalkers do give off warning signals in the early stages of the relationship - bombarding you with messages, phone calls, emails or attempting to control your movements, energy and time.

After the break-up, you may suddenly be finding yourself bumping into your ex at surprising places; or it may be that your ex just happens to be driving by as you find your car has a flat tire as you're leaving for work. It could be that, over the last few days, you've seen him around your area of work. You might suddenly start seeing him at your gym, only to discover he's just got a membership there. You likely think it seems odd or overly coincidental that your ex is turning up so frequently, but you simply shrug it off: maybe you're imagining things, and you can't stop them from going to the same places as you, after all.

Even when our ex is aggressive, dangerous and has a tendency to be violent, it can be so easy to downplay the potential risk that they present. Because some narcissistic stalkers stalked their spouses before the break-up even happened, it can be shrugged off as being more of the same behavior - you find it a nuisance, and it's frustrating, but you don't see it as a huge cause for alarm.

Mutual friends (who, as I recommended before, you cease to have contact with after the break-up) who are in contact with your ex may be unintentionally minimizing their behavior by saying things like, 'Sure, they may have a bad temper, or they may be quick to throw insults, but they're harmless really.'

This is more so the case if your mutual friends weren't aware of the true extent of your ex's controlling, aggressive and toxic behavior during the relationship, and not only is it frustrating for you - it's potentially enabling the narc to up the ante with their post-break-up abuse.

Bear in mind, a stalker is more likely to escalate to dangerous levels when they think they have nothing left to lose - when a narcissist is backed into a corner, with no supply remaining, they're a very dangerous breed.

Safety tip: We all know, deep down in our gut, when something's not right. However, when things happen that are outside of our perception of 'normality' - such as when an abusive ex is doing 'nice' things after you've split—it's easy to put to one side just what our gut is trying to tell us.

It's very easy to lose the sound of our inner voice when situations like this arise. As someone with a narcissistic ex, you need to be especially attuned into your internal self-preservation radar and you must trust your gut. I suggest you begin by keeping a journal of all the strange things that happened with your ex, even if you're hesitant to label them as anything sinister. Even if you feel like you're being needlessly dramatic or imagining nonexistent threats, I implore you to keep a note of these things. It starts a paper trail of events that will come in handy in the event that you need to go down the legal route. It also helps you remember things that have happened, and helps you validate your own recollection of things because you've jotted it down at the time. It's also a way to help you identify any patterns in your ex-partner's behavior; this will undoubtedly come in useful when developing a safety strategy.

Also, avoid playing the role of psychologist towards your ex, instead of protecting yourself. Maybe your ex did have a traumatic childhood. Perhaps they're hurt and upset by the break-up (although I'd like to remind you here - they're not upset because they've lost you - they're upset because they've lost their source of supply; their ego is hurt.) It could be that you think they don't have closure, so you're lenient with their odd behavior. These are not your problems to solve, even if they are true. A narcissist will bank on you getting suckered into playing the concerned psychologist instead of protecting yourself.

Safety tip: Please - let go of any thoughts you might have about helping or figuring out your ex and their emotional state. Stalking isn't something you can resolve by reasoning with the stalker or trying to bargain with them. Believe me when I say, they won't be pacified if you agree to meet with them 'one last time' or for 'closure'.

You will not help their lust for power over you by promising them to 'remain friends.' You can't save them if they threaten to do something to hurt themselves - and more to the point, it's also not your job to 'save them', or protect them. Caving into these kinds of threats only serves to put you in danger. Who knows how to push your buttons more than an ex-lover? A *narcissistic ex* - and they'll push every emotional button to get you back in their clutches.

It is important for you to know what your 'buttons' are yourself so you can best protect yourself from having them pushed. If you're motivated by 'what's best' for your ex, or what'll serve them (even though your ex didn't offer you the same compassion) then remember that the best way to help you can give your ex is a one-time-only, abundantly clear 'we're over,' followed by unbroken silence. Anything else puts you in danger, and it also gives them further narcissistic supply to cling on to.

From my conversations with other survivors, it's a common belief in this community that being a victim of stalking says something bad about the stalkee - that there's something 'wrong' that makes them in some way responsible for the stalking.

Even if you don't feel outright responsible for the stalking, you can often feel to blame in other ways: 'I should have picked up on the red flags at the beginning of this relationship.' Or, 'What's so wrong with me that I'd get involved with someone like that?'

This fruitless and unnecessary guilt, blame and embarrassment you may feel can lead to you suffering in silence. In fact, after discussing stalking with one of my support groups online, many victims felt too 'silly' or 'over dramatic' to report their ex's stalking behavior. Many more stalking victims will totally avoid telling anyone about their fears and uneasiness. They felt too ashamed to tell friends and family, who could have been there to defend and support.

Chapter Six: Disarming The Flying Monkeys

'Flying monkeys' is a term to describe the subservient followers who loyally tread on the heels of the narcissist, supporting and justifying everything they do and say.

Named after the flying monkeys from The Wizard of Oz, like the Wicked Witch of the West's minions, a narcissist's flying monkeys are the brainwashed henchmen they use to carry out their manipulative bidding from afar.

To some, the very idea of flying monkeys sounds immature and unbelievable; the notion that other people are so brainwashed and passive in regard to a toxic narcissist seems most unlikely. However, as you've been involved with a narcissist, you know just how well they can manipulate others to suit their vile needs and wants.

Flying monkeys are most commonly recruited and utilized after a breakup. The narcissist will often charm and manipulate new people in their world, and use them to fluff their ego. Flying monkeys, new and old, will be informed how nasty, horrible, sneaky, crazy, and even abusive you were. As you know, a narcissist won't let the truth get in the way of a captivating story.

These flying monkeys are very likely to be compassionate, very empathic types (as a narcissist preys on), and will feel obliged to be protective and defensive of the narc. They'll offer to help the narc in any way they can, which offers the narcissist an ideal opportunity and platform to keep a sadistic control and power over you.

Flying Monkeys may be influenced into aiding the narcissist by the following:

Spying on you and reporting back

For argument's sake, let's assume that you're the one who left the relationship, and wanted to ensure the break-up was cemented by going no-contact and ensuring you had as much distance from the narc as possible. Your narcissistic ex may know some flying monkeys they can utilize that are in your inner circle, or they may go out and make an effort to purposely recruit some flying monkeys from your social circle. These flying monkeys will be used to report back on your conversations, spy on your social media and online presence.

They'll feed back to the narc just what you're up to - they may even throw a few untruths in there if they think it'll please their narcissistic master. That's an additionally dangerous part of being around flying monkeys.

Avoid this by setting all of your social media profiles as private as you can. For a time, I even temporarily deleted my social media and ensured that when I returned to reinstating my profiles, I was very selective about who I kept as a friend and who I accepted friendship requests from going forward.

Be sure to only accept requests from people who are friends of friends, and question those who have mutual connections with your ex - don't be afraid to ask them what they want, especially if you don't know who they are, and they appear to know your ex. Be on your guard for these types of flying monkeys. You may think that this is a bit paranoid, but remember that you've been through a lot within a narcissist's tight clutches, and you know how traumatic that's been. You're worth that extra effort to keep yourself safe and sound.

Taking these cautionary steps means that you can rest easy about any personal information, private news or gossip about you getting back to your narcissistic ex. Even the most loyal, well-trained minions won't be able to find out anything about you that you don't want anyone to know.

Smear campaigns and gossip

Narcissists and their flying monkeys take gossip to a whole new level with their derogatory smear campaigns. You're the one being talked about, gossiped about and their lies can have the rumor mill going into overdrive - it can really make you feel low and helpless.

Narcissists and their eager-to-please minions are known to engage in juvenile gossiping as a form of bullying, simply in order to 'get' to you. At its core, it's a pathetic, childlike way to behave, but when a narcissist feels jilted or like they're not affecting you enough, thus diminishing their power and control, they may begin a smear campaign.

The basic premise of a smear campaign is to turn other people against you. They do this by lying about the nasty, abhorrent things you've supposedly said or done (things the narc has often done to you), or by using the things that you told them in confidence and exposing them into the public domain.

Their sole intent is to punish you and make you sorry for injuring their ego, and often they do it to proactively paint you as the 'toxic' one before you can get in there before them. Flying monkeys happily assist in this by adding more supportive voices to the chorus of slurs and accusations being hurled towards you.

A resentful ex is very often easily dismissed as such, but if lots of people are repeating the same nasty things about you, spreading it across numerous social circles then people generally take this as truth... if everyone's saying the same thing, then it must be the truth... right?

Often, a smear campaign is executed to involve mutual friends, your own friends and it can even spread to include your own family, who your narcissistic ex has duped and charmed over the duration of your relationship.

This, frustratingly, can begin the deterioration of once-important relationships to you. I know this heartbreaking feeling of unfairness and helplessness; it can feel like you'll never stop feeling as low and lonely as you do during this period.

To tell you to 'rise above' something sounds like a cliched and overdone phrase, but in this scenario, it's a very apt one. Be true to you - don't feel the need and resist the urge to defend yourself.

You know your truth. If others don't right now, so what. Let them be sucked into a game of lies and manipulation; if someone attempts to call you out about vile things you've apparently done to your ex, I suggest you simply express that you hope your ex finds happiness and wish them well in their friendship with them. This way, you're not giving the narc what they want by desperately trying to explain yourself, nor are you wasting your valuable energy on this toxicity.

This will also serve to confuse the monkeys and make them wonder if the information they've been given by the narcissist is really true.

In a nutshell, if you refrain from behaving like the awful, vile person you've been made out to be, they're more likely to confusedly give up and hurriedly fly away.

Don't bank on this happening, but by being decent and not biting at the bait, this may make the flying monkeys snap out of their manipulated state and get them questioning who the narc really is.

Group attacks

This involves a group of the narcissist's flying monkeys working together, trying to convince you that behaving in a certain way is going to be in your best interest.

But: it's actually in their best interest, as well as the narcissistic they're working for.

The best thing in this situation for you is to refuse to react. The important thing here is that you recognize the group attack is the manipulative tactic it is - refuse to comply and don't allow yourself to be dragged in by defending yourself.

A good technique that I found worked well when the flying monkeys are talking, is to ask them to fully explain their stance and their reasoning behind what they're asking of you or telling you. Ask questions, allow them to talk about what they've been told about you, what they think they 'know' about the situation, what they want to achieve by telling you, etc.... but most importantly, don't be reeled into defending yourself or attempt to tell your side of the story.

The mere fact that they've taken immediate sides in something that has nothing to do with them means that they've very little interest in anything you have to say anyway. Why do you want to talk to a brick wall by explaining yourself to someone who's allowed themselves to be used, easily influenced and manipulated by the narcissist?

Let them have their say, then you can let them know that they've clearly come to their own perceptions and conclusions, even though they've never come to you alone to get your side of the story. Their opinions should be invalid to you - because they are. You should let them know this, too, if you feel strong enough. Ensure to do it in a way that means you're not being defensive or attacking them, but rather you're shutting down the entire attack. A disinterest in anything a flying monkey says or does is the best way to get them to disappear.

Remain emotionally disengaged and calm, even if inside you're feeling the complete opposite. The flying monkey's goal is to get you feeling nervous and flustered. By remaining objective and showing little (ideally zero) emotional investment into their words or accusations, then you've got the upper hand over them.

Use the flying monkeys' own energy against them to win the 'fight' they're so motivated to have with you. Tire them out (or rather, they tire themselves out by wasting their own energy) and then calmly walk away. By walking away, you're removing both the narc and their manipulated monkey minions from affecting you further.

I know it's difficult and undeniably painful to do this, especially if the monkeys are your own family members or your close friends, but remember that from now on, you need to take care of yourself - no matter what.

Chapter Seven: Stories Of Survivor Escapes From Narcissistic Relationships

In this final chapter, I'd like to end with some stories of survivors of narcissistic relationships. I know that when I was overcoming the fallout of the break-up from my toxic ex, reading other people's stories and experiences made me feel not so alone. I felt comforted by the knowledge that other people had been where I was at that time, and it put me at ease knowing that you can overcome the tight emotional ties you have with an abusive spouse. It also made me feel better when I would read survivor stories where the victim-turned-survivor would come out of the abuse much bigger, better and stronger. This gave me the inspiration I needed to cut contact with my abusive ex, and push myself into bettering my whole life.

I asked some members of our survivor community to share their own stories, and to my surprise, quite a few volunteered.

Here are some of their responses below; I'll begin with Abby:

Things with my narc ex got slowly worse over time. In the beginning, as is the case with most narcissists, he was fine. He was a charming man, thought of by most as a lovely guy, as thoughtful, and always kind. Looking back now, I can see that he started to chip away at my self-esteem and at my self-confidence really, really subtly. It started with sarcastic 'jokes' that I felt obliged to laugh along with, even though they really hurt me inside. He made those sarcastic jibes in a way that made me feel dumb if I didn't laugh along with him. Of course, these 'jokes' would play on my mind long after he told them, and I'd go over them in my head so many times afterward. Even if it was something seemingly small like my cooking or how my clothes looked, it really did begin to slowly erode my self-esteem.

When I dared to ask him to stop with the jokes and sarcasm and let him know just how much his words hurt me, he would turn on me, and make me feel over-sensitive and like he couldn't be himself in front of me because I 'couldn't take a joke'. No matter what, I was forever in the wrong with him.

To be called an 'idiot', 'boring', 'stupid' or 'dumb' became the norm, and even though they're just words, they cut like a sharp knife every time an insult came from his mouth.

The words rapidly escalated from insulting my intelligence to much worse; he would call me vile, derogatory names that suggested I was sleeping around. Of course, I wasn't, but he gaslighted me so much that I would even have to second guess what behaviors I was doing that gave him that impression. Because of his insecurity, he was very controlling.

The thing about this is, I was a really strong person before I met my ex. I never in my wildest dreams imagined that someone like him could chip away at my confidence and my self-worth. Of course, by the time you take in what's happened, you're in too far with this person. Their grip is so strong, and the emotionally messed-up bond you have with them is too much to bear.

He would always say things to me like, 'you couldn't live without me, I know that', or 'you'll never meet someone like me again'. These things, because they were said so frequently, became something I wholeheartedly believed. I was so scared of being without my ex that I tolerated so much abuse from him. He got violent on occasions too when he thought that his control over me was slipping. To help him have even more control over me, he convinced me that marriage and kids was the best thing for us.

Because I'm from quite a conservative family and background, he knew that divorce would be a certain impossibility for me. It would disappoint my family, and he was so intertwined with my parents and my brother that I just knew they'd all take his side.

My ex was also a serial cheat; I don't know how far the cheating went because he was such a good liar, and because I only had so much evidence in the form of texts and circumstantial evidence, like mascara on his shirt and him smelling of different perfumes. But I do know, a thousand percent, he was unfaithful, multiple times. He enjoyed how this made me feel, even though he denied cheating. I would plead for the truth, but he would dismiss me as paranoid with a smile on his face. It made him feel important that I was so upset.

One time, when I found some incriminating texts on his phone, I was begging for him to tell me the truth. I'd been gaslighted to the point that I had zero grip on reality, and this was my attempt to claw that back. I knew I was being lied to, I just wanted that to be verified. He kept denying and denying, and eventually he got angry because I'd checked his phone. I never knew his passcode to his phone, but I managed a sneak look one day and memorized it. When he went to shower, I took a look. What I found there made me sick to my stomach.

There were numerous texts to other women, phone calls to them when he was supposed to be out with his family, texts of intimate pictures. To add insult to injury, some of these women knew he had a wife, and he would talk about how horrible I was to these women. He'd tell them he was trapped, he was only with me because of the kids and that he would love to start a new life. My world felt like it had ended. I didn't know how to react - I became hysterical. He was backed into a corner, so his natural reaction was to lash out - that night he hit me so hard I woke up with two black eyes the next day. As soon as I got up, I knew he wouldn't let this drop because he was enraged that I'd dared to check his phone. The first thing I did that morning, after checking on my kids and seeing the terror on their face when they saw my bruised face, was to call the police. After three rings, my ex snatched the phone out of my hand and smashed it up.

I felt utterly helpless. For the first few weeks after this, I was still in a daze; still trying to comprehend everything. I couldn't yet think about leaving, my head was all over the place and I didn't know where I could turn with my kids. After a few weeks passed and the dust had somewhat settled (for him at least), I began looking into the kind of relationship I was in. I wanted to see if other people were like me, who didn't have many people around them and had kids to think of. I searched the web, ordered books on my e-reader and read blog after blog on this topic.

To my relief, I discovered lots of resources dedicated to abusive relationships and narcissistic abuse. I looked into the word 'narcissism' and all of the traits fitted my husband's behavior. I was becoming more and more enlightened the more I read. I even began participating in commenting on posts and started to become more involved with the groups I had joined (which is also why you're reading my story; because I plucked up the courage to speak to other victims, too). The more I was reading about narcissism and the experiences of other survivors, the more my inner confidence began to bloom. It wasn't an 'outward' confidence - I didn't let my husband see how enlightened I was becoming. The more awake I became, the more I knew I wanted to pull away from my husband. I knew I had to. It wasn't going to be easy, and I knew I'd miss him and ache for him. But, I had something now that I didn't before: a knowledge of what type of relationship I'd become entrapped in and newfound confidence from the other victims of narcissistic abusers.

About three months after the phone incident, after soaking up all of the information I could, I began my plan. It was a safety plan, and it was there to be utilized when I felt I was able to leave my husband. Slowly but surely, I started to get my things in order. I photocopied my important documents and left them in my drawer at work, along with important numbers and information. I kept my passport somewhere safe and started to save some money. My husband was very controlling with finances, so I could only save a little here and there, but after around six months, it had added up. I opened my own bank account and made sure my statements etc were paperless so my husband wouldn't find out.

I confided in my manager at work and let her know most of my situation. She was someone I felt comfortable talking to, as she'd always been supportive - I suspect she knew I was in an abusive relationship already before I'd told her anything. By telling my manager, I knew if anything more happened, I'd be believed. On top of this, I began keeping a journal of my husband's abuse - times, dates and a paragraph on each incident about what had happened. I kept this little journal in my laptop bag, where I knew he'd never look.

I also confided in a friend about the state of the relationship and agreed with her that we'd have a safe word in case I needed help; for example, if I was in trouble or needed her to come and get me, without alerting my husband, I'd text her the word 'candlestick'. It was random, but it was practical.

Roll on three more months, I was ready. I had things set in place, a pot of money to fall back on and enough evidence to be believed if I needed to involve the police. I had my friend pick up my kids from school, and when I left for work one day, I instead went to pick up the keys to my new place.

Of course, it was hard. My ex tried all the tricks in the book to get me back; the constant contact, the hoovering, the manipulation, the threats, the flying monkeys... sometimes it worked. Until, of course, I couldn't take it anymore. The kids were used by him as a bargaining tool and a way to manipulate me, and I'm grateful they were of an age where they could see what he was doing - they didn't buy into it.

He met someone new, and of course, still tried to get me back every now and then. But, now I'm stronger than he could have ever imagined. He can't touch me in any way at all - and that's the greatest karma of all: knowing how much it kills him, knowing he can't affect me anymore.

Chloe's story:

When you've been in a long term relationship that has been psychologically abusive, it's inevitable you eventually start to believe it. When you decide that you want to get out of it, you don't think you're capable - the abuser has such a hold over you that you feel utterly powerless and like there's no hope. You're afraid of how you'll be treated by others when your ex tells them how nasty and evil you are. It makes it so hard to get out. I was so full of fear and I didn't feel deserving. I felt I wouldn't be taken seriously, seeing as I was never physically abused. I wasn't hit by my abuser. If he had physically abused me, that would have been very crystal clear for me - I would have known what that was - domestic violence.

What was happening to me was so confusing; I wasn't being punched or slapped, but I was afraid. I was made to feel like a nuisance, like I was always ungrateful and undeserving of any kindness or empathy. He would mimic my crying or how I sounded when I was upset. I was told I was a 'snowflake' whose sensitivity was nothing but a huge turn-off for my partner. He had an underlying rage that I was so afraid of - he didn't even need to speak sometimes, just the look on his face told me I should be afraid. He had this grip on me without ever laying a finger on me.

I sought out help after one particular incident. We were in the car, driving to the supermarket. He usually drove, but as he'd drank so much the night before, he was still over the limit, so the driving duties were mine that day. This made me unbearably anxious - he normally drove, and he would scream and yell at me and my 'bad driving'.

He was already moody and agitated because of his hangover, so my driving was something that I knew was going to antagonize that. Sure as the sky is blue, a few minutes into us driving to the supermarket, he began his abuse. He'd scream at me for taking too long to set off after a red light, yell at me for letting too many cars pass at our turning, and he'd smack the dashboard if I was driving too slow. Of course, I was a nervous wreck.

When it came to parking at our destination, I had to back into a pretty tight spot, and whilst I was doing this, he got out of the car and began really screaming at me, as he was directing me into the parking spot. Passers-by looked over, shocked at how I was being spoken to. Some people stopped and stared at my husband, although this didn't deter him from his onslaught of abuse.

When I eventually parked, much to his dissatisfaction, he kept going on at me, following me and yelling obscenities at me as I made my way towards the store. He was hollering the worst insults towards me, and I could feel the spit hitting me as he hissed at me through gritted teeth. He was saying I was stupid, too dumb to function in society, he couldn't believe he was stuck with such a stupid, overweight cow... the insults just seemed to escalate to the most vile things imaginable. I just burst into tears, unable to take the pain of his hurtful words and the humiliation of him doing this in public. He threw his bottled water at me, and the lid came off as it hit me, so my top was soaked. Then he walked back to the car, where he got in and waited for me to drive him back home.

Whilst this wasn't an isolated incident - he'd done stuff like this plenty over the years - it was the incident that finally made me snap into taking back control of my life.

I told a friend about this incident and also opened up about the many others that had occurred over the years. My friend had always thought of my partner as 'odd', but she was shocked to the extent that his verbal abuse, gaslighting and manipulation had gone.

She urged me to call the police, but I felt like they would think I was a time waster or crying wolf. Looking back now, I should have called the police - his behavior was most certainly criminal, but at the time I didn't feel that way. He made me feel like his actions were always justified, and I was certain he would make sure the police thought this, too. Plus, he was seen as respectable and educated, with a 'good job' - I felt like I'd not be able to compete if it came to involving the law, as he worked within that sector.

Instead of going to the police, I looked for someone I could talk to that wasn't my friend. As helpful and cathartic it was to offload to her, I didn't get the understanding I needed in order to fully get things off my chest. She had no understanding of narcissistic relationships. So, as well as joining every forum and group dedicated to narcissistic abuse that I could find, I also spoke to my local abuse charity. At first, I felt utter shame - there were lots of times I had their number on my phone ready to ring, only to hang up before someone answered. I spoke with them one day when they picked up quicker than I could hang up - and I'm so glad they did.

I poured my heart out to an understanding, empathetic and kind lady who I'll always credit my leaving this abusive relationship with. She had also been a victim of an abuser, and she was so soothing to talk to. She offered me lots of advice and resources, as well as letting me know about safe places I could go to. Whilst I wasn't ready to take her up on this offer just yet, I still called up and offloaded every now and then.

I even made a real attempt to make another go of this relationship. It was a last-ditch thing, I think - I just needed proof that he wouldn't ever change, no matter how much I did to please him. The last straw was when I made supper for him and his parents, only for him to insult my 'overdone veg' and 'poor quality' steak as I served up the food. After taking a few bites, he picked up everyone's dish and insisted he wouldn't allow them to eat it - it was inedible. He scraped his and his parents' plates into the bin, leaving me with my plate full. His parents seemed awkward, but almost like they agreed with his shocking behavior - they certainly didn't stop him.

He proceeded to cook everyone else pasta, all the while profusely apologizing for my 'god-awful' food.

I ended up in a refuge a few days after that. I had a bag of belongings and that was it. Whilst you may think this would be the point I would feel lowest, I actually felt liberated; I was free. I may have had next to nothing, but I had my freedom. Everything else - the possessions, the home, the nice things - I could build back up. I needed my freedom, and if I had that, I was capable of anything.

Of course, I still felt for my ex. I fell for a sweet, caring, and loving man-not the vile and toxic person he turned out to be. I mourned for that person - the one that didn't exist. The only connection to him was through my horrible ex. So, there were times when I was hoovered back in. I would often break my own 'no contact' rule, only to block him again hours later. I think I was hoping that, when I reached out, the person who I fell for would reach back. However, every time, it was my abusive ex.

He hacked into my social media account, he called my work to tell them I'd been stealing, he would try to find out where I lived (when I moved on from the refuge) and he would use a mutual friend to check up on my movements.

I ended up moving to another city - not directly because of my abusive ex, but a work opportunity came up and I saw it as a fresh start. It gave me everything I needed to move on: space, a new focus, new people to connect with and the ability to live without fear. Now when I head home to visit friends, I do see him around and I feel nothing. The first few times, my heart pounded and I thought I was going to faint; now when I bump into him at the same bar or restaurant, I look right through him.

He can't affect me. I've got too much self-respect, self-worth and too much going for me to let an insecure, abusive, tortured little man bring me down. In the end, the narc never wins, because all they're left with is themselves: they'll never like who they are, and they have to live with that.

****

And this draws a close to this book. I do hope it's helped you, inspired you, given you new things to think about or offered you some words of comfort.

Do let me know if this has been beneficial for you; you can leave a review, and if you'd like to offer up a little of your own story with it, that would be unbelievably valuable to someone who reads it who's in an abusive relationship.

Here's to being stronger than you ever thought you could be.

Don't miss out!

Visit the website below and you can sign up to receive emails whenever Lauren Kozlowski publishes a new book. There's no charge and no obligation.

https://books2read.com/r/B-A-PTHI-EHVZ

BOOKS 2 READ

Connecting independent readers to independent writers.

Also by Lauren Kozlowski